Who Does This Job?

BELL BOOKS

Wh

Text copyright © 1991 by Pat Upton.
Illustrations copyright © 1991 by Matt Novak. All rights reserved.
Published by Bell Books, Boyds Mills Press, Inc., A Highlights Company,
910 Church Street, Honesdale, Pennsylvania 18431

Publisher Cataloging-in-Publication Data
  Who does this job?; illustrated by Matt Novak; by Pat Upton.
    32p.: col. ill.; cm.
Summary: A simple text with illustrations introduces the farmer, zookeeper, grocer,
doctor, and others to young readers.
A Visual Education Book
ISBN 1-878093-20-7
1. Occupations—Juvenile Literature. 2. Picture-books—Juvenile Literature.
[1. Occupations. 2. Picture-books.]
I. Novak, Matt, ill. II. Upton, Pat. III. Title.
590-dc20   [E]   1991
LC Card Number 90-85722
Printed in Hong Kong
Distributed by St. Martin's Press

Does This Job?

By Pat Upton

Illustrated by Matt Novak

Who grows the corn?

"I do," says the farmer.

Who brings the mail?

"I do," says the mail carrier.

Who drives the bus?

"I do," says the bus driver.

Who feeds the animals?

"I do," says the zookeeper.

Who cooks the food?

"I do," says the chef.

Who collects the train tickets?

"I do," says the conductor.

Who directs the traffic?

"I do," says the police officer.

Who puts out the fire?

"I do," says the fire fighter.

Who sells the vegetables?

"I do," says the grocer.

Who takes care of people?

"I do," says the doctor.

Who teaches school?

"I do," says the teacher.

Who learns in school?

"We do, we do," say the children.

"We all do our jobs here."